DATE DUE

	OCT 1 1 2004	MAY 0 7 2016
AUG - 2 2000	FEB 0 5 2016	
AUG 2 8 2000	MAR 2 2 2005	JUN 0 8 2017
SEP 21 '01	AUG 1 1 2005	MAY 2 9 2018
NOV 0 8	APR 0 1 2006	OCT 2 6 2018
MAR 2 3 2002	MAY	DEC 1 5 2018
APR 0 2 2002	APR 1 2 2011	JAN 2 8 2020
JUN 1 9 20	MAY 1 7 2011	
OCT 2 2 20	SEP 3 0 2011	
NOV 2 0 20	MAR 1 5 2	
DEC 3 0 2003	OCT 2 0 2012	
FEB 1 7 2004	MAR 2 7 2013	
JUN 2 2 20	OCT 0 4 2014	

GAYLORD | | PRINTED IN U.S.A.

Truck Drivers

by Karen Bush Gibson

Consultant:
Rebecka Torn
Manager of Communications
Ontario Trucking Association

Bridgestone Books
an imprint of Capstone Press
Mankato, Minnesota

Bridgestone Books are published by Capstone Press
151 Good Counsel Drive, P.O. Box 669, Mankato, Minnesota 56002
http://www.capstone-press.com

Library of Congress Cataloging-in-Publication Data
Gibson, Karen Bush.
    Truck drivers/by Karen Bush Gibson.
    p. cm.—(Community helpers)
    Includes bibliographical references and index.
    Summary: Introduces the work truck drivers do, the kinds of vehicles they drive,
the training they need, and the people who help them.
    ISBN 07368-0625-3
    1. Truck drivers—Juvenile literature. 2. Trucking—Juvenile literature. 3. Truck
driving—Vocational guidance—Juvenile literature. [1. Truck drivers. 2. Occupations.]
I. Title. II. Community helpers (Mankato, Minn.).
HD8039.M795 G53 2001
388.3'24'02373—dc21   00-028426

Editorial Credits
Sarah L. Schuette, editor; Timothy Halldin, cover designer; Katy Kudela,
    photo researcher

Photo Credits
David F. Clobes, cover, 6, 16
Highway Images/Bette S. Garber, 10, 12, 14
Index Stock Imagery, 20
Jack Glisson, 18
Marilyn LaMantia, 4
Shaffer Photography/James L. Shaffer, 8

1 2 3 4 5 6 06 05 04 03 02 01

Table of Contents

Truck Drivers

Truck drivers drive trucks of all sizes. They transport goods from one place to another. Truck drivers spend most of their time driving on roads and highways.

transport
to move or to carry something from one place to another

What Truck Drivers Do

Truck drivers transport cargo. Cargo is the goods people use. Truck drivers sometimes load and unload cargo. They make sure goods arrive at stores or businesses on time.

What Truck Drivers Drive

Truck drivers drive large or small trucks. Large trucks carry heavy goods such as building supplies. Other trucks pull tanks filled with oil, chemicals, or milk. Smaller trucks carry light goods such as letters and packages.

Different Kinds of Trucks

There are different kinds of trucks. Cement trucks carry and mix cement. Dump trucks move dirt. Cattle trucks carry cows. Car carriers transport new cars. Refrigerated trucks keep food cold. Delivery trucks deliver mail and furniture.

cement

a gray powder mixed with water; people use cement to make objects or to join objects together.

Where Truck Drivers Work

Truck drivers drive on highways and roads. Some truck drivers drive short distances. They go home every night. Other truck drivers drive long distances. These drivers sometimes sleep in sleeper cabs.

sleeper cab
the area in the cab of a
large truck that has a bed

Tools Truck Drivers Use

Truck drivers sometimes use CB radios to talk to other truck drivers. They use computers to find driving directions. Truck drivers use ramps and carts to load and unload cargo. Some truck drivers write down what happens during a trip in a log.

log
a book in which people keep written records

15

Truck Drivers and School

Truck drivers go to truck driving school. They learn about truck safety and how trucks work. Truck drivers have to pass driving and safety tests. They then earn a truck driver's license.

truck driver's license
a piece of paper that gives a person permission to drive trucks

People Who Help Truck Drivers

Truck drivers often work for trucking companies. Managers or dispatchers at the companies tell truck drivers where to deliver goods. Highway workers and police officers also help truck drivers. They work to keep roads safe.

dispatcher
a person who gives messages or directions

How Truck Drivers Help Others

Truck drivers carry important packages to businesses. They deliver medicine to hospitals. They bring food to schools for lunches. Truck drivers transport things people need every day.

medicine
a drug used to treat an illness

Hands On: Make a CB and Talk in Code

Truck drivers have used citizen band radios, or CBs, since the 1970s. They use CBs to talk to other truckers. You can make a CB and talk to your friends.

What You Need

An adult to help
A hammer and a nail
2 empty tin cans
Piece of string
  15 feet (4.5 meters) long
A friend

CB Codes	
10-4	Message received
10-7	Over and out
10-9	Repeat message
10-13	Weather report
10-20	Where are you?

What You Do

1. Ask an adult to make a small hole in the bottom of each can with a hammer and a nail.
2. Thread one end of the string into the bottom of each can. Tie a big knot in each end of the string. Pull on the string so that the knots are tight against the holes inside the cans.
3. Stand across the room from a friend. Make sure that the string is pulled tight and is not touching anything. Talk or whisper into the can while your friend listens.
4. Talk to your friend using the codes listed above. Create your own codes and nicknames.

Words To Know

cargo (KAR-goh)—the contents or goods carried by a truck

cement (suh-MENT)—a gray powder mixed with water; people use cement to make objects such as buildings and sidewalks.

dispatcher (diss-PACH-ur)—a person who gives messages or directions to truck drivers; dispatchers often work for trucking companies.

manager (MAN-uh-jur)—someone in charge of a store or business

transport (transs-PORT)—to move or to carry something from one place to another

Read More

Greene, Carol. *At the Trucking Company.* Chanhassen, Minn.: Child's World, 1999.

Ready, Dee. *Trucks.* Transportation. Mankato, Minn.: Bridgestone Books, 1998.

Schaefer, Lola M. *Tractor Trailers.* The Transportation Library. Mankato, Minn.: Bridgestone Books, 2000.

Internet Sites

Kids Korner
http://www.ontruck.org/kids/index.htm
Safety City
http://www.nhtsa.dot.gov/kids
Ted and Trisha's Truck Stop
http://www.dot.gov/edu/k5/truck.htm

Index